GOD'S GIFT
Sermons for Advent, Christmas and Epiphany
Cycle C Gospel Texts
BY JAMES T. GARRETT

C.S.S Publishing Co., Inc.
Lima, Ohio

GOD'S GIFT

Copyright © 1991 by
The C.S.S. Publishing Company, Inc.
Lima, Ohio

All rights reserved. No part of this publication may be reproduced, stored in a retrieval system, or transmitted in any form or by any means, electronic, mechanical, photocopying, recording, or otherwise, without the prior permission of the publisher. Inquiries should be addressed to: The C.S.S. Publishing Company, Inc., 628 South Main Street, Lima, Ohio 45804.

Library of Congress Cataloging-in-Publication Data
Garrett, James T., 1926-
  God's gift : sermons for Advent, Christmas, and Epiphany : cycle c gospel texts / by James t. Garrett.
    p.   cm.
  ISBN 1-55673-312-7
  1. Advent sermons.   2. Christmas sermons.   3. Epiphany season — Sermons.   4. United Methodist Church (U.S.) — Sermons.   5. Methodist Church — Sermons.   6. Sermons, American.   I. Title.
  BV40.G37   1991
  252'.61—dc20
                                                              90-23417
                                                                  CIP

9133 / ISBN 1-55673-312-7

In loving memory of
Frances Carpenter Garrett

Preface

God's gift of Jesus Christ made possible not just a new way of understanding life but a new way of living life. These sermons were preached to the congregation of Marvin United Methodist Church. Their love and encouragement makes preaching the gospel a challenge and joy each Sunday.

I am indebted to my late wife, Frances, who listened, encouraged, and gave loving support. She was my greatest fan and most ardent supporter and critic. She provided a strong home base that is so important in ministry. She knew the wise devotion that knows how to love deeply without holding on too tightly. Her years were too brief, but what she leaves is a persistent summons to the power and peace of holy living as God's gift.

My gratitude to Mrs. Velma Cole, whose skills and hard work as a secretary, helped make this manuscript possible.

May God help us to use the gifts of life for God's glory and honor and in loving service to others.

James T. Garrett

Table Of Contents

Preface	5
Advent 1	9
Christ Is Coming	
Luke 21:25-36 (C, L)	
Luke 21:25-28, 34-36 (RC)	
Advent 2	13
Prepare The Way Of The Lord	
Luke 3:1-6	
Advent 3	19
He Preached The Good News	
Luke 3:7-18 (C, L)	
Luke 3:10-18 (RC)	
Advent 4	23
The Christmas Song	
Luke 1:39-55 (C, RC)	
Luke 1:39-45 (46-55) (L)	
The Nativity Of Our Lord	27
The First Christmas Message	
Luke 2:1-20	
Christmas 1	31
Home And Temple	
Luke 2:41-52	
Christmas 2	35
The Gospel Of Christmas	
John 1:1-18	
The Baptism Of Our Lord	39
Jesus Is Baptized	
Luke 3:15-17, 21-22	

Epiphany 2 43
Ordinary Time 2
    Jesus' First Sign
    John 2:1-11 (C, L)
    John 2:1-12 (RC)

Epiphany 3 47
Ordinary Time 3
    A Short Sermon
    Luke 4:14-21

Epiphany 4 51
Ordinary Time 4
    Jesus Is Rejected
    Luke 4:21-30

Epiphany 5 55
Ordinary Time 5
    Jesus Said: "Try Again"
    Luke 5:1-11

Epiphany 6 59
Ordinary Time 6
    Luke's Beatitudes And Woes
    Luke 6:17-26

Epiphany 7 63
Ordinary Time 7
    Refuse To Be A Victim
    Luke 6:27-38

Epiphany 8 67
Ordinary Time 8
    The Proof Is In The Fruit
    Luke 6:39-49

The Transfiguration Of Our Lord 71
    A Voice Out Of The Clouds
    Luke 9:28-36

C — Common Lectionary
L — Lutheran Lectionary
RC — Roman Catholic Lectionary

Advent 1
Luke 21:25-36 (C, L)
Luke 21:25-28, 34-36 (RC)
Christ Is Coming . . .

Today is the start of the season of Advent. A season of anticipation. A season of hope and waiting. It is a time of preparation for the coming of Jesus Christ. It has been said: "The extraordinary thing that is about to happen is matched only by the extraordinary moment just before it happens. Advent is the name of that moment."[1]

Jesus shares with his disciples concerning his second coming. An extraordinary thing . . . matched only by the extraordinary moment before it happens. A strange text for the season of Advent; or is it? I think not. The birth of Christ encompasses much more than the Christmas story. Understanding this moves us into a realm which is far more than sentimentality.

The Christmas happening affected the whole universe for all eternity. The eternal God was incarnated in a man named Jesus. Jesus is God's story-word in the flesh. It is a story of the love of God and humanity. Like all stories it has a beginning and will have an ending — a completion, a grand climax.

When Jesus came the first time, he came as a baby in a manger in an obscure village. Nobody much knew or cared except Mary and Joseph, some shepherds and angels. He says he will come a second time.

God works purposefully to build his kingdom — a kingdom of justice, righteousness and redemption. Human needs (good or bad) can never daunt the purpose of God. It is his doing, apart from all human calculation or designing. God is in charge. Write that down — God is in charge!

Jesus tells his disciples, "There will be signs in sun and moon and stars, and upon the earth . . ." There will be signs and circumstances reverberating through the entire universe

Signs, things which will cause us to fear. Some fears are healthy. Dean Martin once quipped: "Show me a boy who does not know the meaning of fear and I'll show you a boy who gets beat up a lot." We're all a little jumpy. Being human means being insecure.

When nothing is left, God is left. God's love will not be defeated. Nothing in this world can separate us from God's love.

Paul writing to the Christians in Rome makes the affirmation: Who shall separate us from the love of Christ? Shall tribulation, or distress, or persecution, or famine, or nakedness, or peril, or sword? Nay, in all these things we are more than conquerors through him that loved us. For I am persuaded, that neither death, nor life, nor angels, nor principalities, nor powers, nor things present, nor things to come, nor height, nor depth, nor any other creature, shall be able to separate us from the love of God, which is in Christ Jesus our Lord.

God never promised a life free from trial. What God promised was to be with us always, and through the grace of Jesus Christ, to give us the victory.

Therein is our hope. In the Book of Genesis we find the story of Noah. There had been endless days on the ark . . . days of waiting and hoping. In every direction Noah could see only water. One day, in faith, he released a dove to search for land. The Bible says the dove "found no place to set her foot" and returned. Noah was put on hold. He had to wait. He waited with faith and in hope.

He sent out a dove a second time. It returned with a spring of freshly plucked olive leaf in its beak. Noah could not see the land, but he knew it was there. It began to appear out of the watery waste. The worst was over. As sure as God made little green apples, a new, green world would emerge out of the wreckage of the old.

In Christ we find a freshly plucked olive leaf pointing toward a day when all tragedy shall be overcome and all pain destroyed. A new heaven and a new earth; for the first heaven and the first earth had passed away. A new kingdom will emerge. This is our faith. This is the mood of Advent.

Time began anew with the birth of Jesus Christ. The Incarnation establishes a new situation for humanity in the cosmos. God's action at Christmas was to be decisive, ultimate, and final.

With the birth, death and resurrection of Christ a whole new world has been created. When anyone is united with Christ, there is a new world. It is a world where Christ rules as Lord, where the Holy Spirit functions to keep life human, where love is the rule.

Our Lord said, "Look up and raise your heads, because your redemption is drawing near."

Frederick Buechner wrote of the ever-appealing Christmas story: As for myself, the longer I live, the more inclined I am to believe in miracles. I suspect if we had been there at the birth of Christ, we would have seen and heard things that would be hard to reconcile with modern science. But that is not the point. The gospel writers are not really interested primarily in the facts of the birth. They are interested in the significance, the meaning for them of that birth.

When a child is born, we who love that child are not interested primarily in the facts of the birth. Rather we are interested in what the birth means to us and how for us the world never will be the same again. Our lives are charged with new significance.

When Jesus was born the whole course of history was changed. The birth of Jesus into the darkness of the world made possible not just a new way of understanding life but a new way of living.[2]

Since his birth, countless different kinds of people in countless kinds of ways have been filled with his spirit. They have been grasped by him, caught up in his life, and have found themselves in deep and private ways healed and transformed in their relationship with him.

He was indeed the long-expected One, the Christ, Wonderful Counselor, Mighty God, Everlasting Father, Prince of

Peace. In this child there is a power of God to bring light into our darkness, to make us whole, to give a new kind of life to anybody who turns toward him in faith. Even to such as you and me . . . he is salvation. He is the gospel of God. Apart from him there is no gospel.

This is the only truth that really matters. The truth of the story is found in the hearts of believers. It is being lived out that it lives.

Take us in, Lord, and give us the shelter of a manger. Break through our darkness with the light of a star. Reach out to our loneliness, and draw us into a family. Open our ears to the choirs of heaven. And take our pain and use it to bring to birth something new! May all the promise, hope, joy and love of Christmas be yours in Christ.

Advent 2
Luke 3:1-6
Prepare The Way Of The Lord

Jeannette Clift George, director of the Houston-based A. D. Players, sent me a copy of her book titled *Travel Tips from a Reluctant Traveler*. It's a delightful book with many helpful tips for the journey of life. In the opening chapter she writes:

"My cousins live in Asheville, North Carolina, where Jesse is a prominent surgeon. He is a fine man, a very gracious man, a very loving man, but a man who doesn't like cats. His wife, Frances, is a delightful person who loves cats.

"One day, a little neighbor girl ran crying to their house. Her cat had climbed up a tall, slender tree and couldn't get down. Jesse thought that was a good place for a cat to be, but following Frances' gentle persuasion, he said, 'Let's see what we can do to help.'

"The two of them decided that Frances, who is of small stature, would grab the lower part of the tree and work it down until the topmost branches reached Jesse. Then Jesse, who is quite tall, would scoop the frightened cat from the top of the tree to safety. Their plan worked well at first. Frances grabbed the part of the tree within her reach and pulled it toward her. The tree tipped down like a thirsty giraffe, bearing a tiny passenger on its head. The branches were almost to Jesse when Frances lost her grip!

"Whoom! The tree slipped from Frances' hands and sprang away with such great force that the cat was flung into space! Catapulted! Claws out! Eyes wide! Approaching a certain but unknown destiny.

The little girl was crushed, but the shock of her beloved cat's mode of departure stopped her sobbing. Frances was overcome by guilt because she and Jesse had lost the little girl's cat. Jesse tried not to laugh . . .

"A few days later, Frances was in the grocery store and noticed a friend pushing a grocery cart with cat food in it. She knew that her friend's husband didn't like cats any more than Jesse did. 'I see you have cat food. Do you have a cat?' she asked.

"Her friend stopped, looked around to be sure no one else could hear, and said that the strangest thing happened. She said that she and her husband were sitting in the backyard when all of a sudden, out of nowhere, a cat landed at their feet! She said that her husband looked at the cat and then at her. He said, "Maude, the Lord has sent us a cat!' "[3]

Jeannette said "the story gives me insight into the dilemma . . . and the bewilderments I often find in life. I identify with that cat!" So can we all.

Sometimes we are flung out into unchartered space — not sure where we're going, but going there very rapidly. There are clashing priorities in our lives. Sometimes we may even look like that cat. Claws out! Eyes wide! Gasping for breath and trying to get our act together before we land.

It can happen to any of us, particularly at this time of year. The pressures of the season can rob you of the meaning of the season. It is easy to take on the coloration of the society in which we find ourselves. There is enormous power in simple things to distract our attention from God. Guard against being swamped by the pressures of this season.

God's Word directs us to make preparations for the coming of the Lord. In Luke chapter 3, verses 1-6 is the voice of the one whom himself was out of unusual birth and a gift from God. John, the son of Zechariah, says: "prepare the way of the Lord."

Much of the joy of Christmas is in the preparation and the anticipation of it. It is this dimension that makes Christmas. Rouse a person on a given morning and say, "It's Christmas!" and even if it is, to that person it is not. They have not anticipated.

In a sense everybody makes preparation for Christmas. We prepare our homes, hang a wreath, put up a tree. We buy gifts and wrap them in beautiful colors. Plan parties, prepare for family gathering, do extra cooking. All of these are important preparations. One of the joys of the season is sharing it with friends and family.

I have no desire or intent to put any of these down — to make you feel guilty about them. They're important preparations that touch our attitudes and our basic emotions.

However, let's not forget to stay with the main event. The main event features a baby in the manger. The Christ Child. Focus on the meaning of his birth for your life and for our world. Let the voice in the wilderness of old speak to us in our wilderness.

The spiritual needs to invade our materialism. Our earthly warrings must be challenged by the Prince of Peace. The sacred needs to penetrate our secularism. The joy of the birth can echo in our despairing hearts.

In the East when a king proposed to visit a part of his kingdom he would send a messenger ahead to tell the people to prepare the roads. John is the messenger of the King. "The King is coming," he announced.

Prepare the way of the Lord, make his paths straight. Every valley shall be filled, and every mountain and hill shall be brought low, and the crooked shall be made straight, and the rough ways shall be made smooth; and all flesh shall see the salvation of God.

Mend not your roads but your heart. Get ready to receive the good gifts of life. Prepare, anticipate receiving all that makes your life rich and colorful and joyous.

Harold Kushner reminds us it is not dying that most of us are afraid of. It's something more unsettling and more tragic than dying that frightens us. We're afraid of never having really lived. It's possible to come to the end with a sense we never figured out what life is for.[4]

Jesus Christ is God's birth to his creation. It is the fulfillment of prophecy. Luke sets the preparation for the advent of Jesus in the context of world history and the universal purpose of God. Christmas is by grace. It could never have happened otherwise. Our gospel is the gift of repentance and forgiveness of sins to Israel and to all people.

The gospel encounters all — everything and everyone. Nothing or no one needs to be outside of the salvation of Jesus Christ. The universality of salvation was in the heart of God always.

God loves us — not because we have deserved his love. He has chosen to love us. Before we loved him, he loved us, as children, through Jesus Christ our Lord.

That's the good news of Christmas! Through Christ one is related to God, the everlasting Father, in an altogether new way, in a way that is similar to adoption. Under the Roman law the old life of an adopted child was completely wiped out. Legally all debts were cancelled; wiped out as if they never existed . . . the adopted person was regarded as a new person entering into a new life with which the past had nothing to do.

An adopted child is a chosen child. Isn't that wonderful! Paul's use of the word shows God's choosing of us. We are his children by his deliberate will. God in his amazing grace and mercy has taken the lost, helpless and weak — adopted them into his own family. The debts are cancelled. The unearned love and glory inherited.

John Killinger has taken some of the parables of Jesus and retold them in the language of Christmas.

What person among you, taking 100 children to the theater for a performance of *A Christmas Carol*, if you lose one of them, does not stand the other ninety and nine in the theater lobby and go in search of the one that is lost? And when you have found the little tyke, you take it in your arms with rejoicing.

And when you get back to the lobby, you say to the others, "Whee, everybody, I have found the lamb who was lost." I tell you, there is more hanging of evergreens in heaven over one sinner who repents than over ninety and nine just persons, who need no repentance.[5]

Prepare the way of the Lord, . . . "No threat. Not a grim warning. A gracious invitation! An invitation to prepare for

Christ to be born anew in your heart. I invite you to receive Jesus Christ into your life. To live your life in his love through his church.

". . . and all flesh shall see the salvation of God."
    Joy to the world! the Lord is come;
    Let earth receive her King;
    Let every heart prepare him room.

Advent 3
Luke 3:7-18 [C, L]
Luke 3:10-18 [RC]

He Preached Good News

Last Sunday we examined the beginning of John's sermon where he said the King is coming, prepare! Today we continue with that sermon. Hear the words of John, the son of Zachariah, recorded in Luke 3:7-18.

John, austere preacher, calls for the multitudes to prepare the way for Christ's coming with severe earnestness. His message is a call to repentance with actions that demonstrate an altered life. "Bear fruits that benefit repentance," he says. "We have Abraham as our father," is not a valid claim or an excuse. A life of faith and deeds of love are what counts before God. A religion void of moral and ethical implication is exactly that, void.

The idea that love is something we do is somewhat foreign to the modern Western mind. We grew up thinking that love is a feeling that overtakes a person. Some don't understand it entails a commitment, concern, and concentration. It is something we are called to do.

It is true what we think and feel influences what we do. It is equally true what we do influences what we think. Our actions condition our thought patterns and determine our feelings. E. Stanley Jones advised: It is easier to act yourself into a new way of thinking than to think yourself into a new way of acting. If we decide to do loving things for people, these actions can generate loving feelings toward those people.

Christmas is not a theological idea. It has to do with flesh and blood events that happened, are happening and will happen. It's truth is discovered in our own stories, what happens in our own lives.

And the multitudes asked him, "What then shall we do?" Bear fruit that benefits repentance: share with others, be honest, avoid violence, act in love, was the reply.

"And Jesus said a certain man, while doing his Christmas shopping, fell among muggers, who stripped him of everything, beat him to within an inch of his life, and left him in an alley behind St. Luke's Church.

"The minister came along on his way to a service, and, when he saw the man, hurried into the church, afraid of becoming involved. And likewise an elder of the church came by and hurried past, as frightened as the minister. He even dropped the holly wreath he was carrying and didn't return to pick it up.

"But the neighborhood agnostic, who didn't even believe in exchanging Christmas presents, when he heard the poor man groaning, investigated and felt sorry for him.

"Bringing his car around, he helped the man into it, ignored the blood on his velvet pile seats, and drove him to city hospital.

" 'Here,' he said to the receptionist, who presented him with a battery of forms. 'This is my credit card, and he is my brother. Give him a private room and the very best of care, and, if it exceeds the limits of my charge account, I'll borrow the money and pay you. What the heck, it's Christmas Eve!'

"Which of these three men, do you think, was neighbor to the man who was mugged? And which one had a merry, merry Christmas?"[6]

An all-time favorite story at Christmas is "The Other Wise Man." Artaban, in his pursuit of finding the newborn King, misses his three friends who set out before him. He misses the Christ Child, too, because his journey led him into strange encounters with dying beggars, and frightened mothers to whom he gives two of his three jewels saved for the Child. He returns to Jerusalem after a fruitless search in Egypt. For 33 years he still searches for the Child.

Now, an old man, Artaban notices an unusual commotion during Passover time. He inquires as to what is happening. "We are going to the place called Golgotha, just outside the walls of the city, to see two robbers and a man named Jesus of Nazareth hanged on a Cross." Artaban knows instinctively this is the King he has been searching for all his life. He rushed to the scene.

On his way he meets a young girl being sold into slavery. She falls at his feet and pleads with him to rescue her. His heart is moved and he gives away his last jewel for her ransom. At that, darkness falls over the land, the earth shakes and great stones fall into the streets, one of them upon Artaban, crushing his head. He lay dying in the arms of the girl he has just redeemed. He says, "Three and thirty years I looked for thee, Lord, but I have never seen thy face nor ministered to thee!" Then a voice comes from heaven, strong and kind, "Inasmuch as you did it to one of the least of my brethren or sisters, you did it to me."

His face grows calm and peaceful. His long journey is ended. He has found the Christ.

Dear friends, don't overlook the old refrains in that story: a journey, obstacles, acts of love, and ultimate grace and redemption and peace. And, don't forget where he found the Lord: in the people who crossed his journey's path.

How we respond to a world that contains so much wrongness, hurt, and despair is very much our responsibility. "Beloved, let us love one another as I have loved you," says Jesus. God is love, and you find that love by loving people. Somebody loving you is grace, your loving someone is grace.

Blessed are they who find Christmas in the age-old story of a babe born in Bethlehem. To them a little child will always mean hope and promise to a troubled world.

Blessed are they who find Christmas in the Christmas star. Their lives may ever reflect its beauty and light.

Blessed are they who find Christmas in the joy of giving lovingly to others. They shall share the gladness and joy of the shepherds and wise men of old.

Blessed are they who find Christmas in the fragrant greens, the cheerful holly and soft flicker of candles. To them shall come bright memories of love and happiness.

Blessed are they who find Christmas in the happy music of Christmas time. They shall have a song of joy ever singing in their hearts.

Blessed are they who find Christmas in the message of the Prince of Peace. They will ever strive to help him bring peace on earth, goodwill to men (author unknown).

The good news of Christmas is:

"He who is mightier than I is coming," said John, "the thong of whose sandals I am not worthy to untie; he will baptize you with the Holy Spirit and with fire."

Teilhard de Chardin once wrote: "Someday, after we have mastered the winds and the waves, the tides, and gravity, we will harness for God the energies of love, and then for the second time in the history of the world man will have discovered fire."

The Christ is coming. What shall we do? Deep within our beings we know . . . we know . . . go and bear fruits that benefit a citizen of the kingdom. And you too will hear a voice from heaven, strong and kind, saying, "Inasmuch as you did it to one of the least you did it to me." Amen!

Advent 4
Luke 1:39-55 [C, RC]
Luke 1:39-45 [46-55] [L]

The Christmas Song

The business side of Christmas — the commercialism — doesn't bother me as it does some. There are those who think the spiritual import of Christmas may be forgotten. There's no danger of that. The spiritual significance of Christmas is so dominant that many who are ordinarily indifferent go out of their way to find a religious service. That is part of the miracle of Christmas.

Personally, the exchange of gifts, the decorations in our homes, and the adding of color to drab streets is not a contradiction to the spiritual importance of the season. These traditions and rituals repeated each year help rekindle in our consciousness what happened a long time ago. They help us recall emotions that otherwise would get lost in the past. The simple fact God has come to be with us in Jesus Christ never grows stale. Visual images help tell the story.

The holiday season is a ritual-filled time. Rituals are important. They build solidarity and generate loyalty. Christmas is a ritual-filled day for most of us. One family has a prescribed ritual for the opening of gifts. A family member goes to the pile of gifts under the tree, picks up a gift and gives it to the person whose name is on the tag. The gift is opened while others look on trying to guess what it is. Then they go through the same ritual with the next gift and so on.

Some of the gifts are wrapped in used paper from a previous year. The mother would always say, "Now save the paper. We'll use it next year." The world is divided into two kinds of mothers: those who save wrapping paper and those who don't.

I cannot explain it, but every year it happens. A special quality of Divine Presence invades our world. It is as if a magic wand is waved over the world and everybody and everything becomes different. Year after year the world in some measure stops to listen to the story.

I love the Christmas music. Christmas has to be sung. Music and song began with the first Christmas. The song of Christmas sung by Mary is found in Luke 1:39-55.

Here is a moving account of the mother of John being visited by the mother of Jesus. A spirit of joy and celebration surrounded the births of both John and Jesus. The scene is an unnamed city in the Judean hills. Upon hearing Mary was to give birth to the Messiah, the babe leaped in Elizabeth's womb. This prenatal activity accents the sovereign will and purpose of God. Elizabeth is inspired by the Holy Spirit and blesses Mary for having been chosen to be the mother of the Lord and for believing and accepting the word spoken to her from God.

Mary's joy and excitement is expressed in a song. She praises God for the favor bestowed upon a maiden of low estate. Her song proclaims the triumph of God's purposes for all people everywhere. All the oppressed, poor, and hungry will be blessed.

"He who is mighty has done great things for me, and holy is his name." sings Mary. Ah yes, that's the song of Christmas — God has done great things, and holy is his name. The song contains the essence of the Christmas gospel:

"My soul magnifies the Lord, and my spirit rejoices in God my Savior, . . . And his mercy is on those who fear him from generation to generation. He has shown strength with his arm, he has scattered the proud in the imagination of their hearts, he has put down the mighty from their thrones, and exalted those of low degree; he has filled the hungry with good things, and the rich he has sent empty away."

At Christmas we celebrate a mighty act of God. God sends the gift of a child into the world. All the conditions of normal human action and achievement are absent. They're not there. It is totally, entirely, completely, absolutely the work of God. The Child is a gift of God's grace.

Of course, every birth is a gift of God's grace. Every child represents a new potential. Each newborn is a sign God has not given up on the world.

The observation has been made that during times of war and destruction the birth rate increases. Is this accidental? Or is it when the processes of men are engaged in destroying life there is One at work more authentic than the design of the human mind?

A new spirit was released into the world with the birth of Jesus. It's a mystery beyond our understanding. He who is mighty has done great things for us.

A little girl, dressed as an angel, in a Christmas pageant was told to come down the center aisle. The child asked, "Do you want me to walk or fly?" You feel as though she almost could have flown. Don't ever lose the wonder and mystery of Christmas.

Every year I'm reminded of those words of the late Peter Marshall: "When Christmas doesn't make your heart swell up until it nearly bursts and fill your eyes with tears and make you all soft and warm inside then you will know that something inside of you is dead."

The mystery of Christmas gave a young virgin a song to sing. This was not to be an ordinary birth but a virgin birth. The birth of righteousness, peace and love in this stern world is always a virgin birth. It is never humanity nor the power of mankind that brings it forth. It is always God! God working in and through those who hear and obey.

The new, the holy is to be born. If the new is to be born, then the old is going to have to give way. There is agony in the process as well as joy. Just as there is agony in the womb as it labors to give birth to new life.

Mary will give birth to a holy, eternal Child. The Child Herod could not slaughter. The Child the Roman Empire could not bury. This is God's Son. The Child who was to be born is the One who may be born again even in us.

O holy Child of Bethlehem, descend to us, we pray; Cast out our sin, and enter in, be born in us today. We hear the

Christmas Angels the Great glad tidings tell; O come to us, abide with us, Our Lord Emmanuel!

On this Sunday before Christmas Day we move closer to the manger at Bethlehem in our journey of Advent. Bethlehem will not be the end of the journey, only the beginning — not home but the place through which we must pass if we are to reach home at last.

May Christmas put a song in your heart.

"My soul magnifies the Lord, and my spirit rejoices in God my Savior.

"He who is mighty has done great things for me, and holy is his name."

Is there a person who is unable to say that? Repeat with me: "He who is mighty has done great things for me, and holy is his name." Amen and Amen!

The Nativity Of Our Lord
Luke 2:1-20
The First Christmas Message

The story of the birth of Jesus as told by Luke is the most familiar to most people. The familiarity of the story can be a frustrating thing for the preacher. Who is capable of rising to an occasion on which the most beautiful text of the Bible is read? It makes the preacher turn pale and stammer.

However, the familiar can be the preacher's delight. That the text and message are familiar means they already belong to you, the listeners. There is power, enjoyment, and an occasional "amen" when we hear what we already know and believe.

The record of Jesus' birth is straightforward. It is told as a historian would relate it, citing date, place, and circumstance. It is an earthly event which came straight out of heaven.

It opens with the decree of Augustus that his whole empire should be taxed. Before the tax could be imposed, there must be a census. Everyone was directed to go to their ancestral home for enrollment. Joseph and Mary went to Behlehem. Joseph was a descendent of King David, whose home had been Bethlehem.

Jesus is to be the fulfillment of prophecy. Luke weaves the old and the new together as one fabric. The Bible tells one story — the salvation of God.

The innkeeper had no room. The Child is born in a manger. And, the shepherds are the first to hear the good news from an angel: . . . behold I bring you good news of a great joy . . . for to you is born this day in the city of David a Savior, who is Christ the Lord.

What a nice touch God adds to the Christmas event. The shepherds were not only poor and powerless, they were despised by the religious orthodox. Their occupation took them into wilderness where they were unable to regularly observe ceremonial religious laws. Yet the temple authorities needed the shepherds. According to the Law they had to sacrifice the unblemished lambs daily. Those who looked after the sacrificial lambs were the first to know and the first to see the true Lamb of God, who "taketh away the sins of the world."

The news of the birth comes first not in a palace hall but in the fields, to the poor shepherds. The shepherds acted immediately. They went with haste to the manger. There they found the babe — a Savior, who is Christ the Lord.

Jesus was born to be the Savior of the world. That was the first Christmas message. It is the Christmas message today. That's what we all really need — a Savior! We want to know forgiveness, salvation, peace with God. A longing both universal and personal. It is ancient and modern. Our whole world needs the Savior.

You have received many invitations during this season but none is more important, or equal to the one sent by God at Christmas. In Jesus Christ each of you has a personal invitation from God with an RSVP. There is evil in the world, but we can rise above it. There is much that is ugly and indecent, but it is possible to live a good life. Death is still with us, grief and sorrow, but death no longer has power over us. New life begins in Jesus Christ.

> *That night when in Judean skies*
> *   The mystic star dispensed her light*
> *A blind man moved amid his sleep*
> *   And dreamed that he had sight.*
>
> *That night when shepherds heard the song*
> *   of hosts angelic choiring near,*
> *A deaf man stirred in slumber's spell*
> *   And dreamed he could hear.*
>
> *That night when in the cattle stall*
> *   Slept child and mother cheek by jowl*
> *A cripple turned his twisted limbs,*
> *   And dreamed that he was whole.*

That night when o'er the newborn babe
The tender Mary rose to lean
A lothsome leper smiled in sleep,
And dreamed that he was clean.

That night when in a manger lay
The Sanctified who came to save
A man moved in the sleep of death,
And dreamed there was no grave.

— *Author unknown*

Not only "that night" but every night since his birth people of faith have been able to dream and live with new hope. It's what makes the good times great and the bad times bearable.

Fred Craddock tells about a trip to his home state of Tennessee. He was in a restaurant in the Smoky Mountains. It was one of those informal places where the proprietor is the waiter, the cashier, and the greeter. He moved from table to table, visiting with the diners. He introduced himself to Dr. Craddock and wanted to know who he was and what he did. Craddock confessed that he was a preacher. The cafe owner pulled up an empty chair and sat down, and began to tell his whole life's story.

The man said that he was born in a little town in Tennessee, not far from where they were. He was born to a mother who wasn't married. It was the kind of town where everybody knows everybody else, what they've done, all the gossip and scandals. They had a name for someone who was born to an unmarried mother, and the boy got used to hearing that name before he even knew what it meant. It followed him to school. On the playground he would hear it from other children. When he went downtown, all looked at him as if he were somehow different from others. His mother wanted him to go to Sunday school, but even the church people seemed to look at him as if they were afraid he might be a bad influence on their own children.

One day a new preacher came to town. The boy went to church. When the service was over he tried to hurry out. The preacher stopped him at the door. He said, "Who are you, son, whose boy are you?" He felt that he would like to crawl into a hole somewhere. The new minister had obviously already heard about him. But before he could answer, the preacher said with a warm smile on his face, "Wait a minute! I know who you are." He leaned down and looked closely into the boy's face and said, "I can see a family resemblance. You are a child of God." Then he put his hands on the boy's shoulders and straightened up and said, "Boy, you've got quite an inheritance. Go out and claim it."

God made Christmas for us. But there is a sense in which all of us have to make our Christmas. All the salvation of God is finished and complete, but it is not mine until I claim it.

No ear may hear his coming,
But in this world of sin,
Where meek souls will receive Him still
The dear Christ enters in.

"A Savior for you is born this day." Tonight, as you take the bread in your hands, let it once again be the sign of your salvation. We are saved, through the life, the death and the resurrection of One born so long ago in a little town called Bethlehem.

You are forgiven. You are loved. Peace on earth and goodwill to everyone. Merry Christmas!

Christmas I
Luke 2:41-52

Home And Temple

Columnist Erma Bombeck tells of a Supermom who is perfection itself. She did everything right: kept a perfect home; kept her husband happy. Always had a copy of Bishop Fulton Sheen's latest book on the coffee table, and answered the door pregnant when the priest came by.

One day, I asked her how she did it, and she said, "I emulate the Blessed Virgin Mary," and I said, "Marge, it's a little bit late for that."

She said, "Very well, I'll tell you. Every evening, when the children are bathed and tucked into their clean little beds, and the lunches are lined up and labeled and packed in the refrigerator, and the little shoes are racked up, and the driveway is waxed, and I've heard all the prayers of the children, I fall down on my knees and say, 'Thank you, God, for not letting me kill one of them today.' "

Jesus died at the age of 33. Of these 33 years he spent 30 of them in a village home in Nazareth. Jesus had his roots in Judaism; a child of a devout home; a child of the synagogue in Nazareth. His parents were conscientious about their religious obligations, and mindful of the traditions of their people.

In Luke chapter 2, verses 41 to 52, we find a childhood experience of Jesus.

Luke presents the home and temple as formative institutions in the development of Jesus. At every point the Law of Moses was kept; circumcision, Mary's purification and Jesus' dedication, and now the family's annual pilgrimage to Jerusalem for Passover.

It all began, for Jesus, in the home as an infant. Ecclesiastes gives these directions: Remember your Creator in the days of your youth, before the evil days come, and the years draw nigh, when you will say, "I have no pleasure in them"; before the sun and the light and the moon and the stars are darkened and the clouds return after the rain.

Remember your Creator when you are young. When you are young, your soul has just come fresh from God. Haven't you observed how naturally small children can talk of God and Jesus? Why? Because they just came from there. But when you have been here for awhile, mowed the grass, bought a car, mortgaged a house, got married, had a few bad experiences you forget whence you came.

Every birth is a sign — a sign God hasn't given up on the world. If we weren't so blind, we might see life itself is sacramental.

To a great extent the success or failure of an individual to live up to his or her uniquely human potential depends on the family background.

Dr. Alan Loy McGinnis, a family therapist and director of Valley Counseling Center in Glendale, California, in an article wrote: ". . . parents, in their devotion to a child, will pull him or her up beside them — and then encourage the child to go even higher."

When Harry and Ada Mae Day had their first child, they traveled 225 miles from their ranch to El Paso for the delivery. Ada Mae brought her baby, Sandra, home to a difficult life. The four-room adobe house had no running water and no electricity. There was no school within driving distance.

But the Days did not allow themselves to be limited by their surroundings. Harry had been forced by his father's death to take over the ranch rather then enter Stanford University, but he never gave up hope that his daughter would someday study there. Sandra's mother first taught her at home, and also saw to it that the house was stocked with newspapers, magazines and books. One summer the Days took their children to all the state capitals west of the Mississippi.

Sandra did go to Stanford, to law school, and became the first woman justice on the U. S. Supreme Court. On the day of her swearing in, the family was there. "She looked around, saw us and locked her eyes right into ours," said her brother, Alan. "That's when the tears started falling."

What motivates a woman like Sandra Day O'Connor? Intelligence, of course, and inner drive. But much of the credit goes to a determined ranch mother sitting in her adobe house, reading to her children by the hour, and who, with her husband, scampered up the stairways of capitol domes, their children in tow.

The home has a decisive influence in the shaping of character and beliefs.

However, I feel the need to add something more . . . humans have the ability to overcome the destructive effects of poor upbringing, provided there has been no physiological damage. For we can learn how we should behave. We all know persons who have "made good" despite a terrible childhood, even, perhaps, because of it — steeled and tempered by hardship, determined to prove him or herself.

Jesus' lingering behind in the temple is a testimony to the deep faith of the family. It is the fulfillment of the act of giving the child Jesus to the Lord. Jesus now claims for himself that special relation to God which was symbolized in his dedication as an infant.

In the sacrament of infant baptism we ask: Will you endeavor to keep this child under the ministry and guidance of the Church until he/she by the power of God shall accept the gift of salvation, . . . ?

Jesus was nurtured, from birth, in the faith. At age 12 there were in him the vague stirrings of his own uniqueness. Twelve years old — already, the stirrings are there.

If we come to God late we miss much good that we could have enjoyed had we been more fortunate. It cannot be helped when it happens that way, but it is not all the same whether we come to him soon or late.

When St. Augustine finally gave himself to God he wished it were not so late in the day. "Too late have I loved thee, O thou beauty of ancient days yet ever new!" He wrote. He was 32 years of age.

Christmas 2
John 1:1-18

The Gospel Of Christmas

A wife gave her husband two ties for Christmas. He, being an obedient and peace-loving man, went immediately and put on one of the ties. He returned to the kitchen where his wife was preparing breakfast. Seeing he had one of the ties on she asked: "What's the matter, don't you like the other tie?"

Through the Advent season we read Luke's story of the coming of the Lord and of his birth. These weeks leading up to today, Christmas, we have made preparations. We have anticipated with great expectancy the birth of Jesus Christ. When we gathered to light candles in celebration of his birth, the light was taken from the Christ candle and passed to each worshiper. This sanctuary became a sea of candlelight, in a solemn but joyful affirmation that light came into this world in the birth of Jesus our Lord. Finally, Christmas has arrived. What meaning does all of this have for our lives and for our world?

Only God could have dreamed Christmas.

"In the beginning was the Word. And the Word became flesh and dwelt among us, full of grace and truth: we have beheld his glory, glory as of the only Son from the Father."

Christmas had its beginning long before Joseph and Mary, and in a place beyond Bethlehem. The Word was "with" God, "in the bosom of " God. What God was, the Word was. He is not man becoming God but God Incarnate, God coming into human flesh, coming into from outside.

In other ways and in other times the eternal word came into the world, only to have the door slammed in disbelief. Now a new and marvelous move has been made. The Word has come in flesh to live among us and to make God known to us.

God's attempt to love and redeem the world will not be thwarted.

Kierkegaard has a fable of a king who fell in love with a maid. When asked, "How shall I declare my love?" his counselors answered, "Your majesty has only to appear in all the glory of your royal raiments before the maid's humble dwelling and she will instantly fall at your feet and be yours."

But it was precisely that which troubled the king. He wanted her glorification, not his. In return for his love he wanted hers, freely given. Finally, the king realized love's truth, that freedom for the beloved demanded equality with the beloved. So late one night, after all the counselors of the palace had retired, he slipped out a side door and appeared before the maid's cottage dressed as a servant.

Clearly, the fable is a Christmas story. We are called to obey not God's power, but God's love. God wants not submission to his power, but in return for his love, our own.

God moved in. He pitches his fleshly tent in silence on straw, in a stable, under a star. The cry from that infant's throat pierced the silence of centuries. God's voice could actually be heard coming from human vocal cords.

That's the joy of it. God has come to be with us. Nothing in this world can separate any of his children from his love.

Not even our prodigal rebellions, nor our adult indifferences; our sins nor our sufferings. No experience goes unattended by God. Cradles of insecurity — he is there; deserts of temptation — he is there; gardens of indecision — he is there; crosses of suffering — he is there. He is in them all. This is the God of Christmas!

"And the Word became flesh and dwelt among us, full of grace and truth." That's the word I most need to hear today. Grace! God touching the brokenness of my life, giving strength and encouragement when I need it the most. God giving to me that which I need and taking from me all of those things I don't need.

Oswald Chambers wrote: "There is only one relationship that matters, and that is your personal relationship to a personal Redeemer and Lord. Let everything else go, but maintain that at all costs, and God will fulfill His purpose through your life.'"[7]

One of the best known parables of Jesus has been retold in the language of Christmas by John Killinger. The parable is the gospel of Christmas.

"A certain man had two sons. The younger one said to his father, 'Give me my Christmas presents early this year. I am bored with this place and am splitting for the big city.'

"And the father took the presents out of the closet and gave them to him.

"And not many days after, the son packed his bag and took a long trip to the city, where he wasted all his money in an endless round of Christmas parties. He even hocked his father's presents, and soon he had spent all that, too.

"The minute he had run out of funds, doors were closed to him and the party spirit was over. In desperation, he went out and attached himself to the owner of a Jewish delicatessen, who sent him into the kitchen to wash dishes. He was so hungry that he sneaked scraps of food off the plates he was cleaning. And no one said as much as a kind word to him.

"Finally, on the day before Christmas, he came to his senses. 'How often,' he thought, 'have I seen my father set hired help down to a steaming meal at my mother's table, and I am stuck here eating this garbage! I am going to hightail it out of here and return home as fast as I can, and I will say to my father, "Dad, you were right, it's a tough world, and I didn't make it. You don't owe it to me at all, but I would like to come him and work for you as a hired hand, if you'll have me." '

"He turned in his apron, collected the few dollars that were coming to him and went directly to the bus station. All the Christmas lights seemed to blink warmly, as if they approved what he was doing, and the Santas on the street corners blessed him on his way.

"He rode all night, rehearsing his speech as he went. 'Dad, you were right, it's a tough world. . . . Dad, you were right, . . .'

"At dawn on Christmas day, the bus pulled up outside the bus stop in his little hometown, and he tumbled off, wrinkled, unshaven, and a little worried about how it would be.

" 'Son!' a voice called. And there was his father. 'But, Dad, how did you know?' he stammered.

" 'How did he know?' said the old station agent, taking the morning papers off the bus. 'Why, he's come down here two, three times a day, every day since you've been gone.'

" 'Dad,' said the boy, 'It's a tough world, and you were right . . . .'

" 'I know,' said the father, putting an arm around the boy's shoulders. 'Come, let's go home.'

"At home, he called for his wife and anybody else who was in the house and said, 'Look who's here! Look who's here!'

"And he brought out presents and laid them before his son, including a beautiful new bathrobe, a pair of nice leather slippers, and a handsome, sparkling ring.

" 'Here,' he said, putting the ring on his son's hand. 'Go take a nice, warm shower, and put on this robe and these slippers, and come down and we'll have a wonderful visit.'

" 'Get out that standing rib roast we have in the freezer,' he said to his wife. 'And turn on the tree lights! We're really going to have a celebration today!' "[8]

Welcome home this Christmas. The watching is over. New life has begun. God is with us full of grace and truth. Thanks be to God for his unspeakable gift in Jesus Christ our Lord.

The Baptism Of Our Lord
Luke 3:15-17, 21-22

Jesus Is Baptized

Jesus began his public ministry in a crowd that surrounded John the Baptist, at the Jordan. John was a fiery young preacher who attracted the crowds. He told people what they had to do as well as what they had to be.

When John emerged from the desert preaching repentance and baptism, the people flocked to the Jordan to be baptized. He was baptizing everyone who would change their ways. Jesus stepped forward to be baptized. Why would the sinless One be baptized?

Jesus was there to provide the fullness of salvation John preached. He came to identify with the new gospel of salvation for all people — Jew and Gentile. He is the One who will separate the wheat from the chaff. The One who will baptize with the Holy Spirit. Jesus Christ is the new beginning . . . He is salvation.

Look carefully at what happened: "the heaven opened," which was a signal from God of the launching of a new age. A dove flying in the sky above descends upon Jesus. The Holy Spirit is not to make Jesus the Son of God — Luke affirmed that in the birth story. It is the anointing for public ministry. The coming of the Holy Spirit is to empower the servant for his task. And, a voice says, "Thou art my beloved Son; with thee I am well pleased."

Jesus' baptism was a sign of identification. It is still the same for you and me. It is a sign for the acceptance of the love and salvation of Christ. The water baptism identifies us with the family of God, the Body of Christ, the Church. The technique used matters about as much as whether you pray kneeling or standing. It symbolizes the end of everything about your life that is less than human and the beginning in you of something strange and new and hopeful.

In John Bunyan's *Pilgrim's Progress,* Christian arrives in his journey at the palace. The palace is heavily guarded. It will be a battle to seek an entry. A man sits at the door to take the names of those who would dare to enter. Many are hanging back, reluctant and afraid. Christian with a very stout countenance walks up to the man saying, "Set down my name, sir."

"Set down my name, sir." In essence that is what Jesus did when he came to be baptized by John. He especially wanted baptism to identify himself with us human beings. His baptism was not for cleansing from sin, but it was an opportunity to declare himself a part of our humanity, in our needs, as well as in our potential glory.

"Set down my name, sir." This is what baptism is: setting down our name and life on the line for the kingdom of God.

An ancient Chinese proverb advises: "If we do not change our direction, we are likely to end up where we are headed."

Standing on the threshold of a new year may be the proper time for us to examine and sift our values. It's possible that the strongest thirst of our being is still unrecognized, still hiding under this or that. We all live much of life superficially.

None of us are here by chance. We have a purpose, a calling beyond the self, a unique responsibility to decide and act.

Kierkegaard spoke of the "leap of faith." He was speaking of a commitment more dependent on faith than on proof. We are never capable of having all the answers. Those who would grow take many a step, even in the midst of tragedy, not knowing exactly what comes next.

Life calls us to move, to act, to make a commitment, to take a risk, to forge into new territory, trusting God to effect the consequences.

Can you imagine where we would be if Christ has demanded proof of the resurrection before complying with the crucifixion?

But Christ did not make such a demand before he made his commitment. He trusted the future to God. Even with his last breath, "Father, into thy hands I commit my Spirit."

The battle is lost or won in the secret places of the will before God, never in the external world.

I believe in the power of regeneration, a God-given capacity for making a new start in Jesus Christ. Everyone is capable of change.

Human nature is adaptive, and capable of change. No matter however inadequate a human being may be, that doesn't relieve a person from the responsibility of making oneself over into what he should be — a warm human being capable of love and decency.

Those easy evasions: "You can't change human nature," "the leopard cannot change its spots," "you can't teach an old dog new tricks," and the like, are false.

Human nature isn't something that is fixed and inflexible. While it is true the leopard cannot change its spots, we can certainly change ours.

The American educator, Horace Mann, described the predicament of habits saying: "Habit is a cable; we weave a thread of it every day, and at last we cannot break it."

Mr. Mann, you are only half right. Habit is a cable; we weave a thread of it every day, but it can be broken? There is One who will help you break it, if you desire it. Habits are often practiced without guilt, justified through cleverly devised mental schemes.

We have to be continuously converted all the days of our lives, continually to turn to God as children. Life is a continuous conversion. In every setting in which we are put we have to "put on the new person."

There are whole areas of our lives which have not yet been brought into subjection, and it can only be done by this continuous conversion.

Frederick Buechner reminds us that God cannot be expressed but only experienced. "A Christian is one who points at Christ and says, 'I can't prove a thing, but there's something about his eyes and his voice. There's something about the way he carries his head, his hands, the way he carries his cross — the way he carries me.' "[9]

There is not a single shoe in this place that does not contain a foot of clay . . . a foot that drags; a foot that stumbles; a foot that hurts; and on just such feet we all seek to walk the journey of life.

The only hope we have is Jesus Christ. He is the same yesterday and today and yes, forever. When you need him, he is there. He's there even when you don't think you need him.

Leave the irreparable past in God's hands. Step out into the irresistible future with him. He is our hope; and without him, we would be hopeless indeed.

I offer you a new start in Jesus Christ. I invite you to commit your life to him in the fellowship of his church.

Epiphany 2 (C, L)
Ordinary Time 2 (RC)
John 2:1-11 (C, L)
John 2:1-12 (RC)

Jesus' First Sign

A bonus in being a minister is that I get to share in a lot of weddings. Weddings are joyous and happy times. In the service of marriage are these words: . . . we are gathered together in the sight of God, . . . to join this man and this woman in holy matrimony; . . . which holy estate Christ adorned and beautified with his presence in Cana of Galilee.

It was a wedding in Cana of Galilee that Jesus does his first "sign." The story is told in John 2:1-11.

Weddings then, as now, were great and grand occasions. Friends and family came from miles away; the poor relatives and the rich relatives, the eccentric aunts and the harried uncles. Jesus was a guest at this wedding in the town of Cana.

In Galilee a newly married couple would hold open house for a week. This week of festivity was a high moment in the life where there was much poverty and hard work. To run out of food and wine would be a terrible embarrassment.

In the midst of the festivities a crisis occurred — the wine had run out. Mary informs Jesus of the situation. Jesus has the servants to fill six stone jars with water. He then tells them to take a cupful to the steward of the feast. As soon as the steward tasted it, his whole face lit up. It wasn't water anymore. It was wine. What's more, not just a common, garden-variety wine either. With eyes as big as saucers, the steward said: "Why, usually people serve the best wine first and save the cheap for later. But you have saved the best till last."

This is a story of much deeper meanings than are on the surface. It must be read on a symbolic level and not merely on a story level. Every gesture, every detail suggests a meaning beyond the obvious.

Jesus was at the wedding. He came to share life with people. He entered into their daily lives. He wept at their funerals and rejoiced with them at their weddings. He was perfectly at home at a wedding feast. He was no severe, austere killjoy. He enjoyed sharing in the happy occasions. Once he used a wedding as a parable for the kingdom of God.

He went that day, not to perform a miracle, but simply to be with friends. We all need friends who share with us in life's sorrows and joys.

A writer dedicated a book to a friend with these words: "Duddley Knott was a friend of mine. Some friends are more or less replaceable with other friends, but he was not. He was an Englishman of great style, elegance, wit, and one of a kind. He could make you laugh till you cried. He had a tender heart."[10]

The Country Parson defines a friend as someone who has found in you qualities others have overlooked.

When Harry Truman was thrust into the presidency at the death of FDR, Sam Rayburn gave him some fatherly advice.

"From here on out, you're going to have lots of people around you. They'll try to put a wall around you and cut you off from any ideas but theirs. They'll tell you what a great man you are, Harry. But you and I both know you ain't."

When Sam Rayburn discovered that he was quite ill, he announced to the House of Representatives he was going home for medical tests. Some wondered why he did not stay in Washington where there were excellent medical facilities. He supplied the answer when he told Congressman Jim Wright, "Bonham is a place where people know it when you're sick, and where they care when you die."

Jesus put great emphasis upon friendship. He ministered to his friends and was ministered to by them.

"The mother of Jesus said to him, 'They have no wine.' " Sometimes the wine runs out for all of us. We face shortages in life — a shortage of courage, of wisdom, of strength, or of faith. Many times quitting may be the easiest thing to do.

It is seldom noted that Babe Ruth missed and missed and missed the ball. In fact, he struck out 1,330 times, a record in futility unapproached by any other player in the history of baseball. But what people remember is that he hit 714 home runs, a record unequalled for 40 years. Someone once asked him the secret of his success at the plate. He replied, "I just keep goin' up there and keep swingin' at 'em."

In Numbers there is an incredible story. Israel is at the border of the Promised Land. The land was in sight to be claimed by an obedient faithful people.

God directed that spies be sent into Canaan so the people might taste and see God's goodness and fully understand his work. Israel's spies found the land richer than they had dreamed it would be. They chopped down a branch with a single cluster of grapes, so large it took two men to carry it on a pole between them.

The spies returned to Moses and the people of Israel, announcing: "The land certainly does flow with milk and honey, and this is its fruit." All was as God had promised it would be.

Nevertheless, there is always a human "nevertheless." The spies told of seeing strong people and fortified cities. "We saw the inhabitants of the land as giants and saw ourselves as grasshoppers."

Caleb and Joshua urged the people to move as God had directed. "Let us go at once and occupy it; for we are well able to overcome it," said Caleb.

Nevertheless, the pessimistic report from the other spies caused them to form a committee to quit. And, you know what? God let the quitters quit! He abandoned Israel to wonder aimlessly in the desert until the unbelieving generation died off. They quit and lost the promise of God. Only Caleb and Joshua would live to lead the new generation into the Promised Land.

"Do what he tells you," said the mother of Jesus to the servants. Obedient, faithful people receive the power of God in the midst of human shortages.

Jesus met the need that day and more with six 30-gallon stone jars — 180 gallons of wine. No wedding party could drink that much wine. No need on earth can exhaust the grace of God. There is superabundance in the grace of Jesus Christ. Grace always does more than expected.

Look at the symbolism. The miracle involved six stone jars which held the water for the Jewish rites of purification. The number six meant incompleteness, as the number seven meant completeness.

Jesus took an imperfect vessel for purification and used it as a sign for the new wine of the gospel of grace. The steward of the feast pronounced the new wine better than the wine they already had.

In Jesus there is a new gospel of grace, new wine, new life, vivid, sparkling, exciting. Jesus is the One who has come to give the new wine of the kingdom of God.

That is the story of the wedding at Cana. He "manifested his glory" the gospel says, "and his disciples believed him."

A miracle, just as a miracle trembles on the threshold of taking place in every believing heart.

The glory of Christ is the power of Christ to adorn and beautify, to transform and hallow, the human heart. May he work that most precious of all miracles in us all.

Epiphany 3
Ordinary Time 3
Luke 4:14-21

A Short Sermon

During Advent and Christmas we examined Luke's account of the birth of Jesus. The first Sunday of the new year we watched as the young parents brought the Child into the temple. There in the temple was an old man, whose name was Simeon. He takes the baby from Mary and cradles him in his own arms. Holding the baby close, he says: "Lord, now let thy servant depart in peace . . . mine eyes have seen thy salvation."

Only a few days old and already one has taken him into his heart and claimed his salvation.

From the temple we went to the Jordan where John, the baptizer, is preaching repentance and baptism. Jesus is there to provide the fullness of salvation John preached. He identifies with this new gospel of salvation for all people by being baptized himself. It is the launching of a new age.

Following his baptism, Jesus goes into the wilderness to be alone. There he faces temptations. He emerges from the wilderness victoriously. He returns to Nazareth where he was brought up.

In his home town church Jesus reads the Scripture lesson. When he was through, he rolled up the scroll and gave it back to the attendant and sat down. He looked around, and then said quietly: "Today this Scripture has been fulfilled in your hearing." That was all.

It was a short sermon!

At Christmas I received as a gift the book, *Holy Sweat*, by Tim Hansel. I enjoyed it very much. He tells of a guest preacher in a rather large church who began, "There are three points to my sermon." Most people yawned at the point. They'd heard that many times before.

But he went on. "My first point is this. At this time there are approximately two billion people starving to death in the world."

The reaction through the congregation was about the same, since they'd heard that sort of statement many times before, too. And then he said, "My second point . . ."

Everybody sat up. Only 10 or 15 seconds had passed, and he was already on his second point? He paused, then said, "My second point is that most of you don't give a damn!"

He paused again as gasps and rumblings flowed across the congregation, and then said: "And my third point is that the real tragedy among Christians today is that many of you are now more concerned that I said 'damn' than you are that I said two billion people are starving to death." Then he sat down.

The whole sermon took less than a minute, but it is in many ways one of the most powerful ones ever given. He was reminding us we are called not to mere piety but to genuine morality. We are called to action, not to fancy words.

Jesus preached a short sermon. But what a sermon. He clearly denotes the kind of ministry he came to pursue. It is to be a ministry to the poor and outcast, the blind and unaffirmed.

Jesus made a bold claim that day. I am the Christ! Salvation has become real, visible today.

This was not what they expected to hear. The Scripture goes on to record: "When they heard this, all in the synagogue were filled with wrath. And they rose up and put him out of the city." The good news was bad news.

We've heard all sorts and varieties of good/bad news stories. One is about a man who goes to see his doctor. The doctor says, "There's some good news and there's some bad news." The patient says, "Well, doc, give the good news first."

"The good news," the doctor says, "is that you have 24 hours to live." The patient gasps, "If that is the good news, what is the bad news?"

"Well, the bad news," the doctor continues, "is that I couldn't reach you by phone yesterday."

Jesus said, God "anointed me" to preach good news to the poor, to proclaim release to the captives, recovering of sight to the blind.

When it comes to the good news of salvation all of us are charity cases. We can do nothing but hold up our little tin cups to the only One who can fill it. Martin Luther's last written words were: "We are all beggars."

Jesus saves . . . saves whom? Saves Joe, saves Charlie, Ann, saves me, saves you — just the names without any Mr. or Mrs., without any degrees or titles or Social Security numbers, just who we are, no more, no less.

The captivity referred to is moral and spiritual. Is it true we're slaves? Can we be slaves, we who of all people are so much our own masters? And the answer, of course, is that we're slaves precisely because we are our own masters.

The most blind were not those whose physical eyes were sightless. It was a moral and spiritual blindness.

At our better moments we are appalled by the culture we have created. Imagine archaeologists, some 1,000 years hence, unearthing the movies and plays and television we watched, pouring over the books we read, hearing the music we heard — rock music, hard rock, punk rock, and the kinds of horrors that fascinated us on the evening news.

Now, of course, they would discover we've had our good times too, our blessed times. There have been moments when we've been brave and wise and kind. Every once in awhile a word was spoken that gave us back our lives again. Maybe we even spoke such a word ourselves. Now and then we've had our vision of the people we might be.

Ralph Waldo Emerson made the observation: "An institution is the lengthened shadow of one man." Take that thought — the institutional church is the lengthened shadow of one Man — Jesus Christ. We Christians owe it to ourselves and to the world to resurrect this message of Christ from the debris of history.

Colin Wilson, a provocative writer, wrote: "Human beings seem to have an extraordinary capacity for being deluded by their emotions, so their 'convictions' are usually a mass of unexamined prejudices.''

In Christ hangs the destiny of us all. "Come to me," is how he put it. Christ is not a way of escaping the world but of loving the world, and beneath all the horror, of being loved by him.

Bob Pierce, founder of World Vision, lived by the motto: "May my heart break with the things that break the heart of God."

That is the gospel. Jesus is the good news of salvation, release to captives and recovering of sight to the blind.

"Today this scripture has been fulfilled in your hearing." Today, not tomorrow. Not next year. Today.

May the power of the Holy Spirit touch our hearts and make them receptive to his grace, the freedom and the healing he offers today!

Epiphany 4
Ordinary Time 4
Luke 4:21-30

Jesus Is Rejected

Jesus is in the synagogue on the Sabbath day at Nazareth. He stood there in the center of all those who knew him. He was a hometown boy, the center of attention that day. "The eyes of all in the synagogue were fixed on him" says Luke. From the prophet Isaiah, Jesus reads these words: The Spirit of the Lord is upon me, because he has anointed me to preach good news to the poor. He has sent me to proclaim release to the captives and recovering of sight to the blind, to set at liberty those who are oppressed, to proclaim the acceptable year of the Lord. Jesus closed the Scriptures, gave it back to the attendant, and sat down.

The Word of God is not always pleasant to hear. It does not massage the status quo at the expense of the truth. People don't want their turf invaded, not even by a hometown boy. Walter Bagehot once wrote, "one of the greatest pains to human nature is the pain of a new idea."

The citizens of Nazareth were the favored people and they resented Jesus taking God's Word of grace to others beyond Nazareth, especially to Capernaum. After all, Capernaum was heavily populated by non-Jews.

Israel had been full of widows in Elijah's day, yet Elijah went to the house of a widow in Sidon. Also, Israel had many lepers in Elisha's time, yet Elisha had given the blessing of God to a man from Syria. These stories were quite familiar and part of their tradition. But grace for all was not what they expected to hear from one who was one of them. Most prophets do not get a good hearing in their own country, or popular acceptance during their own lifetime.

Dr. James Sutherland Bonnell, a Presbyterian minister of another generation, has a great line on this text. "Jesus was favorably received by his townsfolk until he challenged the provincial, racial prejudice. He dared to declare that the children of Israel were not special favorites of God. Indeed, the heavenly Father had singled out individuals in Sidon and Syria for unparalleled blessings. "And that," Dr. Bonnell wrote, "really set the heather on fire!"

The people became angry and set out to do away with Jesus. It has been said, people defend nothing more violently than the pretenses they live by. The people in Nazareth fell into the error of thinking to destroy Jesus would also destroy the word of truth. They failed to understand that truth is indestructible!

Coretta Scott King has reminded us that the forces of repression and brutality can slay the dreamer but not the dream.

What the people heard that day was not what they wanted to hear from "their" Messiah. What about "our" Christ? We still reject the biblical Jesus. We want to re-create Jesus in the image of a white, Anglo-Saxon, Protestant Republican. There is often a wide discrepancy between the Jesus of Scripture and the Jesus propagated in American culture.

Fast Lane magazine conducted a survey in which people were asked whose lives they would most like to emulate. Lt. Col. Oliver North was placed first, President Reagan second, and actor Clint Eastwood third. Jesus Christ tied for fourth place with Chrysler chairman Lee Iacocca.

This Scripture directs us to deal honestly with ourselves. Senator Paul Simon, in an interview printed in *U. S. News and World Report* said:

"The great sermons my father preached were not from the pulpit. My father stood up when they took the Japanese Americans away from the West Coast at the beginning of World War II. He took a very unpopular stand. I would love to tell you that I stood up for my father and was very proud of him, but I remember being embarrassed by what he had done. Now, it's one of the things I'm proudest of my father for. And it taught me a great lesson. If you believe something, stand up."

I do not always agree with Dr. Benjamin Spock. But I do admire him. I respect him for his public stand in his convictions even when they may not be popular. In an essay he writes:

"I got my most basic beliefs — in the sense of unthinking attitudes rather than rational credos — from my stern, moralistic, unyielding mother. She wasn't all grim, though. She had a great sense of humor, was a hilarious mimic, and was as invariably charming to outsiders as she was severe with her children. Her scorn was withering. When during World War I my parents decided that, to help conserve wool, I would wear one of my father's cast-off suits, almost black, floppy, cuffless, the exact opposite of what youth were wearing, I cried out, 'Everybody at school will laugh at me.' My mother said fiercely, 'You ought to be ashamed of yourself for worrying about what people will think. Don't you know that it doesn't matter what people think as long as you know you are right.' Of course, at age 15, when peer pressure is enormous, I didn't believe her. Nevertheless, I got some comfort from her words 50 years later when I fould myself indicted for my opposition to the Vietnam War."

It doesn't matter what others think as long as you are right. To be sure, it may cause rejection. You may find yourself in the midst of controversy but Jesus handled the controversy by walking through it.

Jesus Christ is the way, the truth and the life. In Christ hangs the destiny of us all. He is the way, the way out, the way home, the only way that matters. We reject him at our own peril.

At a performance in the Kennedy Center, Julie Harris was portraying the life of Emily Dickinson. Emily talked about religion — about her father's strict Puritan moralism, about the preachers of her childhood who made her feel "guilty, guilty, guilty," and about her growing disenchantment with organized religion. But she also talked about Jesus Christ and her love for him. "I do believe," she said, "that no person can be truly happy until that person can say, 'I love Christ.' "

Emily is right. When you think about it, that's what it's all about, isn't it? Entering into a love relationship with the One who is in all and beyond all.

"Come to me," is how Christ himself says it. Christ is not a way of escaping the world but of loving the world. We are to come to him even though the world calls us in a hundred different directions.

A poem by an unknown author sums it up well.

> *To laugh is to risk appearing the fool.*
> *To weep is to risk appearing sentimental.*
> *To reach out for another is to risk involvement.*
> *To expose feelings is to risk exposing your true self.*
> *To place your ideas, your dreams, before a crowd is to risk their loss.*
> *To love is to risk not being loved in return.*
> *To live is to risk dying.*
> *To hope is to risk despair.*
> *To try is to risk failure.*
> *But risks must be taken, because the greatest hazard in life is to risk nothing.*
> *The person who risks nothing, does nothing, has nothing, and is nothing.*
> *They may avoid suffering and sorrow, but they cannot learn, feel, change, grow, love, live.*
> *Chained by their attitudes, they are a slave, they have forfeited their freedom.*
> *Only a person who risks is free.*

Epiphany 5
Ordinary Time 5
Luke 5:1-11

Jesus Said: "Try Again"

Here is the good news for today from Luke 5:1-11. This is the Word of God! A word of great encouragement and hope. Hope is the unique signature of the Christian gospel. What makes a Christian a Christian is this inability to quit hoping. A new gift from God is at work on our behalf, at all times in all circumstances.

The crowds had pressed Jesus right up to the edge of the water at the Sea of Galilee to hear the Word of God. There he came upon three defeated men. They had fished all night and had only an empty boat to show for their efforts. They had worked hard but had failed. It was a terrible, horrible, no good, very bad day.

Alexander and the Terrible, Horrible, No Good, Very Bad Day is a children's book. It's one of my favorite books of theology. It's about a little boy for whom nothing goes right. The story opens with these words:

I went to sleep with gum in my mouth and now there's gum in my hair and when I got out of bed this morning I tripped on the skateboard and by mistake I dropped my sweater in the sink while the water was running and I could tell it was going to be a terrible, horrible, no good, very bad day . . . I think I'll move to Australia.

In the car pool Mrs. Gibson let Becky have a seat by the window. Audrey and Elliott got seats by the window, too. I said I was being smushed. I said, if I didn't get a seat by the window, I'm going to be carsick and throw up. No one ever answered. I could tell it was going to be a terrible, horrible, no good, very bad day.

And, that's just the way it turned out. That night the little fellow said, "It has been a terrible, horrible, no good, very bad day. My mom says some days are like that. Even in Australia."

Irwin Shaw wrote a short story called *The Eighty-Yard Run*. As a college freshman, at his first football practice, he broke loose for an 80-yard touchdown run. His teammates looked at him with awe. His coach said, "You're going to have quite a future around here." His girlfriend awarded him with a kiss after the practice. Irwin Shaw has the feeling that life is completely satisfying and rewarding.

But nothing in the rest of his life ever lives up to that day again. His football experience is equally disappointing. His marriage sours. The pain of failure is even greater because he remembers thinking on a perfect day many years before that life would always be that pleasant, satisfying and rewarding.

Life does not stand still. There isn't a once-for-all experience. It was Winston Churchill who said, "Success is never final. Failure is never fatal. It is courage that counts."

There are going to be bad days. Sometimes we are going to fall on our respective faces. These failures don't have to be endings. They can be the avenue to experience God's grace more widely and more deeply.

Jesus of Nazareth gets into the boat with the three defeated men. He sat down and taught the people from the boat. When he had ceased teaching, he said to Simon, "Put out into the deep and let down your nets for a catch." Put out into the deep our lives are often fenced in by low expectations. The worst sin is to aim too low.

Many years ago Oswald Chambers said to a group of students in a college chapel service: We have to learn to make room for God — to give God "elbow room." We calculate and estimate, and say that this and that will happen, and we forget to make room for God to come as he chooses . . . Expect him to come, but do not expect him only in a certain way. At any moment he may break in . . . Always be in a state of expectancy, and leave room for God to come as he likes.[12]

Life is anything but predictable! Human nature is not fixed and settled. We live under hope. That hope is rested in God, not the situation.

At the outset Simon is reluctant — "We toiled all night and took nothing!" The words of a person who has already made the effort and failed. Why should he want to put himself in the position of failing again? How useless this all seemed.

Many times quitting is the easiest thing to do once the challenge has lost its glamor in tedious endurance. But to his credit, Simon was willing to take the risk. ". . . at your word I will let down the nets," he replied.

To their utter amazement, there was churning of the waters as the nets were drawn up, with all the silver bellies flip-flopping in the air and spraying foam everywhere. There was such a catch that they had to signal the men in the other boat to come and help them. Now both boats were loaded with fish.

No matter how many times a person has failed there is always the chance that the next attempt will succeed. "Victory belongs to the most persevering," said Napoleon.

I can't explain it but I know there are powerful kinds of good that can come into a life of a person who continues to trust, and love, and holds on.

Simon Peter saw beyond the miracle. He realizes the holiness of the One in his boat. He gets a glimpse of the power and knowledge of Christ. He falls before Jesus saying, "Depart from me, for I am a sinful man, O Lord."

Now, we come to the real meaning of the story. There's more to life than "full nets." One can have full nets and still have an empty life.

Jesus said to Simon, "Do not be afraid; henceforth you will be catching men." When they brought their boats to the land, they left everything and followed Jesus.

You and I have been put on this earth for a more important purpose than to just beef up somebody's mailing list.

In Jesus Christ, God loves more than we can mess up. He wants us to return that love. The same power that caused Simon to fall at Jesus' feet, lifts him into God's service. What a lesson!

Three defeated men moved from empty nets to a full life by the power of Jesus Christ. Jesus invites you to follow him.

When you say yes to that invitation, you, too, will discover how much he has to offer. Launch out into the deep and let down your nets and follow me. You'll be amazed at what God will do.

Epiphany 6
Ordinary Time 6
Luke 6:17-26

Luke's Beatitudes And Woes

The Beatitudes are familiar to us. We have heard them many times. Someone gave me an interesting article about the Beatitudes. It is titled: "The Lesson."

"Then Jesus took his disciples up the mountain, and gathering these around him, he taught them saying:

" 'Blessed are the poor in spirit, for theirs is the kingdom of heaven. Blessed are the meek. Blessed are they that mourn. Blessed are the merciful. Blessed are they who thirst for justice. Blessed are you when you suffer. Be glad and rejoice, for your reward is great in heaven. Remember what I am telling you.'

"Then Simon Peter said, "Do you have to write this down?'

"And Andrew said, "Are we supposed to know this?'

"And James said, "Will we have a test on it?'

"And Phillip said, 'What if we don't know it?'

"And John said, 'The other disciples didn't have to learn this.'

"And Matthew said, 'When do we get out of here?'

"And Judas said, 'What does this have to do with real life?'

"And the other disciples likewise.

"And Jesus wept."

We still have not learned the lesson. Jesus reverses the standard of value around which his kingdom is built. His love is radical, embracing everyone. Behavior is the natural expression of an inward goodness. You do as you believe. You believe as you do. Write that down and mull it over for a little while. You do as you believe. You believe as you do. Oswald Chambers in his devotional writings says, "The characteristic of a disciple is not that he does good things but that he is good in motive because he has been made good by the supernatural grace of God."[13] The kingdom of God is not a place, but a condition.

Today we turn to Luke's set of Beatitudes. They differ from those in Matthew's gospel. Matthew lists nine beatitudes, while Luke provides only four. Then Luke follows them with four "Woes."

Dr. Fred Craddock has suggested there are times when it seems altogether appropriate and important and valuable for the church to gather and plan to do nothing else but to be instructed in the Word of God. He's correct. The Bible is God's Word to us, not a writing we may change to suit our fancy or to appeal to some group in the church. The Bible alone sets the lifestyle of a Christian.

We should come together for no purpose other than to let the Word itself inform us; to let the Word broaden our understanding; to let the Word tap the source of values and beliefs. It is important to let the Word put us in touch with matters eternal and final. And, to be blessed in the reflection upon the Word.

There are some biblical texts which should be read and left alone, says Dr. Craddock. Texts to be released into the room and let them do their work. To let them speak for themselves. To let them introduce us into a world of values and experiences about which we don't talk very much.

The Beatitudes cast their blessings into the room. They say their words. The blessing goes to anyone in reach of it. Hear the Word of God. Luke 6:17-26:

> *Blessed are you poor, for yours is the kingdom of God.*
> *Blessed are you who hunger now for you shall be satisfied.*
> *Blessed are you that weep now, for you shall laugh.*
> *Blessed are you when men hate you, and when they exclude you and revile you and cast out your name as evil, on account of the Son of Man. Rejoice in that day, and leap for joy, for behold, your reward is great in heaven.*

In direct contrast, Luke continues:

> *Woe to you that are rich, for you have received your consolation.*

*Woe to you that are full now, for you shall hunger.
Woe to you that laugh now, for you shall mourn and weep.
Woe to you, when all men speak well of you for so their fathers did to the false prophets.*

Notice how scattered upon all of us are those blessings and woes.

The blessed: the poor, the hungry, the sad, the oppressed and scorned whom the world pushes aside with contempt or cruelty, are within the compassion and eternal love of God. He will right their lot.

The woes: those who are content to satisfy only their physical needs will experience a terrible "famine." Not a famine of bread, not a thirst for water, but a famine of the soul. We who have so much may no longer be eager for the gifts of God. We do not hunger for the invisible because the visible possessions seem to be enough. Thus, the interior world's needs go untended. Jesus remarked one day that for us who have so much to get to Heaven is about as easy as for a Cadillac to get through a revolving door.

The Beatitudes of Jesus contain no imperatives, no exhortation, no "let us go and do," no "oughts," no "musts," except by implication. It's there! They bring us into the realm of the true and the valuable, the eternal and the good.

As always in the presence of the true, the right, and the eternal; we feel the imperative. We hear the command. It's like being in the presence of somebody of extraordinary value, someone whose life counts for something. You know people like that. To be in their presence makes a difference. The world will be different because they lived. They don't have to say what we should do. We know it. We feel it in their presence.

We leave their presence feeling small and guilty and restless. We purchase a little peace by promising ourselves that tomorrow our life will amount to something. It will amount to more than dealing with those questions what shall we eat, and what shall we drink, and what in the world are we going to wear?

Bob Waters, minister at College Station United Methodist Church, tells of a little oak tree in his front yard. Well, it was little, but it's growing like a weed now. It's the third one planted in the same spot. Upon moving into the parsonage at College Station, someone convinced his wife there ought to be an oak tree in that spot. She never gave up on the notion. Bob managed to mangle a couple of her efforts with the lawnmower. She threatened him about this third one, even as Bob told her over and over the tree wasn't going to grow in that spot. The tree took root. It grew broad and leafy after a couple of years. One day someone came by and said, "You know that thing would grow a lot quicker if you would prune some of the lower limbs." So, they did that. The tree has just leaped up quickly. The reason for its great growth is the pruning — the removing of some of the branches that were sapping its energy and contributing nothing to its height or beauty.

Jesus taught us to prune down, so we have energy and wisdom enough "to be" as well as "to do."

Jesus follows the Beatitudes and Woes with a suggestion:

> *Do good to those who hate you; bless those who curse you; pray for those who abuse you; to the one who strikes you on the cheek offer your other cheek; and as you wish that others would do to you, do so to them.*

You take the initiative . . . You take control of your life; don't let someone else determine it for you . . . Don't let the world squeeze you into its mold.

God's love mirrored in human beings is a superior level of living. It reaches out to all without ulterior motivation or the expectation of any return . . . But the Bible promises an intoxicating joy. They will eat and laugh at a great feast!

Epiphany 7
Ordinary Time 7
Luke 6:27-38

Refuse To Be A Victim

When a person enters into any society or any fellowship, he takes upon himself the obligations to live a certain way, by certain standards. If the person fails to live the kind of life necessary, he hinders the purpose of the society.

Once we make the claim that the gospel of Jesus Christ is true then a claim is put on our lives. In today's Scripture lesson, Jesus sets down behavior patterns for kingdom people.

No one needs to go to a Bible commentary to understand this text. It is a Word that challenges and instructs us. It calls into account and puts us in touch with matters that are eternal and final.

The old religious law had deteriorated into mere legalism. Jesus found the old law unsatisfactory. There had to be a new garment. The old garment could not be patched. The new wine could not be put in old wineskins. His teachings are clearly different from any other. He reverses the standards of value around which society is built. God is full of grace and the final work of grace is to make us gracious.

This Scripture deals with those who are victims. They are victims of mistreatment: hate you, curse you, abuse you, strike you, take your cloak and beg from you.

Have you noticed that much of Jesus' teachings are addressed to victims? Perhaps he talked a lot about victims because they came close to him. They heard in his voice, saw in his face a sympathy and understanding. They found him also to be a victim. He knew what it was to have someone spit in his face. He knew what it was to be cursed, to be lied about, to be mistreated, to be slapped, to be mocked, to be nailed on a cross. Jesus knew what it was to be a victim. He was a kindred spirit.

We are all victims. Some are victims of a painful marriage, an unhappy home life. There are those who are victims of parents who are overbearing and demanding. Some are victims of children who are overbearing and demanding.

A man commented: "Who says that kids are rebellious, self-centered, and don't listen to their parents? Last year I told my kids not to spend their money buying me an expensive Father's Day present — and they didn't."

There are those who are victims of disease, prejudices and terrible injustices in the world. Others are victims of age. The Country Parson made the observation: "Old age is when you don't care what folks say about you — if they'll only say something."

We are victims of computers. Have you ever tried to get a bill straightened out? All you get is that the computer has it mixed up and we'll get it straightened out month after month after month.

Everybody is a victim. And, one can develop a victim mentality. We can use it as a means of being excused. "After all look at what he has been through . . ." to be excused from responsibility.

Such an evasion is a denial of that dignity and worth that belongs to the fact we are created in the image of God and recreated in Christ Jesus. There is a quality of dignity and worth and value we must not deny. A victim but refuse to be a victim!

You can always take the initiative. You can take control of your life. Do not reciprocate; do not let those who would victimize you determine your behavior, said Jesus. You take charge of your life and its situation by taking the initiative in loving, caring and giving.

When someone does you wrong, it's his problem.

When you return wrong for wrong, then you have a problem. When we are hurt, how do we respond? For most of us, the answer is quick and easy. We fight back. Negative forces generate negative forces. You shout at me, I shout at you. You muscle me, I muscle you. You hold me down, and sooner or later I will bite your hand.

It was well-known that Lady Astor and Winston Churchill had a running battle most of their lives. One day Lady Astor said to him, "If you were my husband I would poison your tea." To which the quick-witted Churchill replied, "And if I were your husband, I'd drink it."

Something in all of us says, "right on." This is how we feel about little slights, hurts, digs, isn't it?

Look at the gentle Nazarene. Oppressed by hate, he responded with grace. He didn't fight and he didn't give up the cause either. He simply changed the pattern. He met opposition with quiet confidence. He responded to power with peace. And he overcame malice with a gentle touch and a genuinely caring attitude. "But Jesus, didn't they take your life?" "No, no one took my life. I gave my life. I gave my life."

All human behavior is a matter of selected alternatives. "Selected alternatives " . . . We choose how to respond. Ours is the choice no matter what the situation may be.

Paul O. Sand, at a National Conference of Christians and Jews, quoted: "Do More . . ." by John H. Rhodes.

Do more than exist — Live.

Do more than touch — Feel.

Do more than look — Observe.

Do more than read — Absorb.

Do more than hear — Listen.

Do more than listen — Understand.

"Be merciful, even as your Father is merciful, says Jesus. Judge not . . . forgive . . . give . . . "For the measure you give will be the measure you get back."

By the standards of the world, those teachings appear to be unreasonable, irrational, and foolish. But, the foolishness of Christ will still save the world. Paul, in 1 Corinthians, writes, "The word of the cross is folly . . . but the foolishness of God is wiser than man, and the weakness of God is stronger than men."

Clara Barton, founder of the American Red Cross, was reminded by a friend of a cruel thing someone had done to her years before. Miss Barton seemed not to recall it. "Don't you remember it?'' her friend asked. "No," was the reply, "I distinctly remember forgetting it."

Viktor Frankl, a Viennese Jew, was interned by the Germans for more than three years. Later writing about that experience in a book *Man's Search For Meaning,* he said: Occasionally I looked at the sky, where the stars were fading and the pink light of the morning was beginning to spread behind a dark bank of clouds. But my mind clung to my wife's image, imagining it with an uncanny acuteness. I heard her answering me, saw her smile, her frank and encouraging look.

A thought transfixed me: for the first time in my life I saw the truth as it is set into song by so many poets, proclaimed as the final wisdom by so many thinkers. The truth — that love is the ultimate and the highest goal to which one can aspire. Then I grasped the meaning of the greatest secret that human poetry and human thought and belief have to impart: the salvation of man is through love and in love.

The final summary is the "golden rule" given by Jesus. It covers all cases: "And as you wish that people would do to you, do so to them."

Epiphany 8
Ordinary Time 8
Luke 6:39-49

The Proof Is In The Fruit

Oswald Chambers in the daily devotion book titled, *My Utmost For His Highest,* wrote: God expects my personal life to be a "Bethlehem." Am I allowing my natural life to be slowly transfigured by the indwelling life of the Son of God? God's ultimate purpose is that his Son might be manifested in my mortal flesh.

A Christian is a person who is in Christ and in whom Christ dwells. This indwelling experience results in a new lifestyle.

In the sixth chapter of Luke, verses 39 through 49, Jesus underscores the inseparable union of what one is and what one does.

Here is an example of the humor of Jesus. If you have any doubts that God has a sense of humor, look in the mirror! It must have been with a smile that Jesus gave the parable of a person with a log in his eye trying to extract a speck of dust from someone else's eye. We have no right to criticize unless we ourselves are free of faults. That means we have no right to criticize . . . "There is so much bad in the rest of us that it ill becomes any of us to find fault with the rest of us."

This tragicomical scene of looking always to others, not self, becomes a veil protecting us from honest soul-searching. People defend nothing more violently than the pretenses they live by.

A quip published in the *Arkansas Baptist* says, "Some people think they are big shots just because they explode."

Many wounds are inflicted because someone's dissatisfaction with life must express itself. The one who happens to be near enough to be hurt is simply unlucky.

Psychologists tell us two factors account for criticism: one is the secret intent to hurt, the other the desire for superiority.

The act of criticism gives us temporarily a superior position and feeds our confidence. It becomes a means of elevating oneself.

The 250th anniversary of John Wesley's Aldersgate experience has revived our interest in his life. But even he was not without fault.

Wesley often rode on horseback to Methodist gatherings. One day on a narrow path he met an arrogant man, also on horseback, coming in the other direction. The man refused to budge, saying, "I shall not give the road to a fool."

"But I will," replied Wesley, calmly turning his horses off the road.

A historian, after a careful study of Wesley's life, was convinced the Methodist Church would never have spread so fast had Wesley gotten along with his wife, a very difficult woman. He said Wesley was constantly taking to the road, preaching, as much to get away from his wife as to convert the wicked. She was, he said, Wesley's "thorn in the flesh."

In an imperfect world, criticism and moral superiority can come easily. The judgmental approach costs nothing and is worth as much. To hunt for ways to praise others can do far more good. It has been said, "A compliment is verbal sunshine." Praise awakens hope and the desire to be. Mark Twain once remarked: "I can live for two months on one compliment."

"Each tree is known by its own fruit," said Jesus. Behavior is the natural expression of the basic self. A person's life cannot be evaluated in any other way than by his behavior. It's comical to expect figs from a thorn bush, or to pick grapes from a bramble bush.

We have an inside where we live and move and have our being as well as an outside of flesh and bone. Our actions and our words transmit something of the life we have inside us. What one is, one does.

Remember the story of the plainly dressed Mennonite who was stopped on the street by a young convert who asked, "Brother, are you saved?" the long-bearded Mennonite did not respond immediately, but pulled out a piece of paper and wrote on it. Then he handed the paper to the stranger and said, "Here are the names and addresses of my family, neighbors, and the people I do business with. Ask them if they think I'm saved. I could tell you anything."

Writing about "righteousness," Frederick Buechner tells of an exasperated piano teacher saying to a student: "You haven't got it right!" He is holding his hands the way he's been told. His fingering is exceptional. He has memorized the piece perfectly. He has hit all the proper notes with deadly accuracy. But his heart's not in it, only his fingers. What he's playing is a sort of music but nothing that will start voices singing or feet tapping. He has succeeded in boring everybody to death including himself.

Righteousness is getting it all right! If you play it the way it's supposed to be played, there won't be a still foot in the house or a voice not singing.

In the book, *The Little Prince*, the little Prince tells the Fox, "That which is essential is invisible." Take that home with you: "That which is essential is invisible." Essential and invisible . . . we can't see it. We can't handle it. We can't measure it or put our arms around it.

But, in real life, we do see it. It is measured and handled, for Jesus said: "The good man out of the good treasure of his heart produces good, . . . for out of the abundance of the heart his mouth speaks."

Ah, even words, sooner or later, reveal character just as surely and naturally as the fruit announces the kind of tree bearing it.

A married couple was having problems. In a counseling session the wife blurted out, "I can't remember the last time he said, 'I love you.'" His retort was, "When I married you 28 years ago I told you that I loved you, and I said that if I ever changed my mind I'd let you know."

Once Jesus told of a man who was liturgically correct. He stood in the proper place, said his prayers. His form was impeccable. But his heart wasn't in it. The prayers were words to impress others. Another man that day did everything wrong. He stood far back, and just mumbled mercy, mercy, mercy. And his prayer was heard, and answered!

Jesus Christ makes the heart pump faster and louder than anyone else. Open your heart to him, invite him to come into your life. It's a wonderful day when it dawns upon you that you are a child of God, adopted into his family by the love and grace of Jesus Christ. And you begin to live and speak as his child.

"Take my life, and let it be consecrated Lord, to Thee."

The Transfiguration Of Our Lord
Luke 9:28-36

A Voice Out Of The Cloud

Today we celebrate the Transfiguration Of Our Lord. We will soon begin the Lenten Journey. Often Lent is abused. It has in certain times and places become a period of empty abstinence from tidbits of affluence, and the enjoyment of gloom of self-denial.

This is not the purpose of Lent. These 40 days should be a period of engagement with God, of repentance and prayer and a renewal of our baptismal vows. Lent looks towards God's act in the cross and the resurrection. Lent is the opportunity to move within the shadows of the cross and let the heart be bathed with God's love. Lent is a time to look toward the victory of Easter and the victory that is ours in Jesus Christ.

About a week after Jesus' question, "But who do you say that I am?" and Peter's confession, "The Christ of God," Jesus goes up on a mountain to pray. A strange and mysterious thing happens.

I invite you to turn with me to the ninth chapter of Luke's gospel. I shall begin the reading at verse 28 and read through verse 36.

Jesus took Peter, James, and John to a high mountain. He went there to pray. Prayer was vital for Jesus — most especially on occasions of critical significance. Jesus had to make a decision. He went up on the mountain to seek guidance through prayer.

The very Spirit that fed the life of Jesus Christ will feed the life of our spirits.

While Jesus was praying he was transfigured. The appearance of his countenance was altered, and his raiment became dazzling white.

Suddenly two men, Moses and Elijah, appeared in glory and talked with Jesus. They spoke of his death on the cross in Jerusalem. The event is crowded with meaningful symbolism.

Biblical faith takes history very seriously because God takes it very seriously. God took it seriously enough to bring it and to enter it and to promise that one day he will bring it to a serious close.

Moses and Elijah represent the Law and the prophets. Jesus is the fulfillment of the law and the prophets. God's purposes have been long in unfolding. God's servants have been many. Moses and Elijah appearing with Jesus says that the anticipated Messiah is fulfilled in Jesus. As Moses had led the Israelites out of Egypt to form a new nation, Jesus was to lead his followers into a new kingdom. As Elijah had confronted the evil prophets of Baal on Mount Carmel, Jesus was to conquer sin on Mount Calvary.

Moses and Elijah disappeared, leaving only Jesus. The old is ended. The new has come.

Peter is so overwhelmed by what he has seen he wants to perpetuate this marvelous moment by building three altars. Jesus refused the offer. He tells him to be silent about the experience until after the resurrection. Apart from the cross the full story cannot be told. There is one more mountain to climb — Calvary!

Again, as at his baptism, Jesus receives the confirmation of God. Out of a cloud comes a voice saying, "This is my Son, my Chosen; listen to Him!"

Jesus the Christ — a life invested with heavenly light and power for the salvation of the world.

All the way down the 20 centuries since Jesus was born, there have been countless different kinds of people who in countless different ways have been filled with his Spirit. People who have found themselves in deep and private ways healed and transformed.

In the book, *Unconditional Love,* Father John Powell tells of a young man, Tommy, a student in his class, The Theology of Faith. Tommy turns out to be the "atheist in residence" in the course. He constantly objected to, smirked at, or whined about the possibility of an unconditionally loving Father-God.

At the end of the course he asked in a slightly cynical tone: "Do you think I'll ever find God?" Powell decided on a little shock therapy. "No!" he said. "Oh," Tommy responded, "I thought that was the product you were pushing." I let him get five steps from the door and then called out: "Tommy! I don't think you'll ever find him but I'm absolutely certain he will find you!" He shrugged a little and left my class and my life.

Later, I heard a report that Tom had graduated, and I was duly grateful. Then a sad report, Tommy had a terminal illness. Before I could search him out, he came to see me.

"Tommy, I've thought about you so often. I hear you are sick."

"O yes, very sick." . . . "Can you talk about it?"

"Sure. What would you like to know?"

"What's it like to be only 24 and dying?"

"Well, it could be worse." "Like what?"

"Well, like being 50 and having no values or ideals, like being 50 and thinking that booze, and making money are the real 'biggies' in life."

"But what I really came to see you about," Tom said, "is something you said to me on the last day of class. I asked you if you thought I would ever find God and you said, 'No!' which surprised me. Then you said, 'But he will find you.' I thought about that a lot, even though my search for God was not at all intense . . . at that time.

"One day I woke up, and decided to spend what time I had doing something more profitable. I thought about you and your class, and remembered something else you said: 'The essential sadness is to go through life without living. But it would be almost equally sad to go through life and leave this world without ever telling those you loved that you had loved them.' So I began with the hardest one, my dad.

"He was reading the newspaper when I approached him. 'Dad?' 'Yes, what?' he asked without lowering the newspaper. 'Dad, I would like to talk with you.' 'Well, talk.' 'I mean, it's really important.' The newspaper came down three slow inches. 'What is it?' 'Dad, I love you. I just wanted you to know that.' The newspaper fluttered to the floor. Then my father did two things I could not remember him ever doing before. He cried, and he hugged me. It felt so good to be close to my father, to see his tears, to feel his hug, to hear him say that he loved me.

"It was easier with my mother and little brother. We shared things we had been keeping secret for so many years.

"Then one day I turned around, and God was there. Apparently, God does things in his own way and at his own hour.

"But the important thing is that he was there. He found me. You were right. He found me even after I stopped looking for him."

"Tommy, you are saying something very important and much more universal than you realize. You are saying that the surest way to find God is not to make him a private possession, a problem-solver, but rather by opening yourself to his love."

My dear friends, the surest way to find God is opening yourself to his love in Jesus Christ. We can open our hearts to the love of Christ and say, "In peace that only thou canst give, with thee, O Master, let me live." This is the invitation to all today. An invitation from Jesus, whom God said: "This is my Son, listen to Him!"

Footnotes

1. Frederick Buechner, *Whistling In The Dark*, Harper & Row, Publishers, San Francisco, 1988, p. 3.
2. Frederick Buechner, *The Hungering Dark* (Seabury Press, 1969), p. 53ff.
3. Jeannette Clift George, *Travel Tips From a Reluctant Traveler,* Thomas Nelson Publishers, Nashville-Camder, Kansas City, 1987, pp. 13-14.
4. Harold Kushner, *When All You've Ever Wanted Isn't Enough,* Summit Books, New York, 1986, p. 156.
5. John Killinger, *Parables for Christmas,* Abingdon Press, Nashville, 1985, p. 59.
6. John Killinger, *Parables for Christmas,* Abingdon Press, Nashville, 1985, pp. 11-12.
7. Oswald Chambers, *My Utmost for His Highest,* Dodd, Mead & Company, New York, 1935, p. 335.
8. John Killinger, *Parables for Christmas,* Abingdon Press, Nashville, 1985, pp. 63-65.
9. Frederick Buechner, *Wishful Thinking,* Harper & Row, Publishers, New York, 1973, p. 32.
10. Frederick Buechner, *Whistling In The Dark,* Harper & Row, Publishers, New York, 1988, P. 1X.
11. *The Courage of Conviction*, edited by Phillip L. Berman, Dodd, Mead & Company, New York, 1985, p. 167.
12. Oswald Chambers, *My Utmost for His Highest,* Dodd, Mead & Company, New York, 1935, p. 25.
13. Oswald Chambers, *My Utmost for His Highest,* Dodd, Mead & Company, New York, 1935, p. 206.

www.ingramcontent.com/pod-product-compliance
Lightning Source LLC
Chambersburg PA
CBHW060853050426
42453CB00008B/961